Ocean Friends

PORPOISES

Sebastian Avery

PowerKiDS
press.

New York

Published in 2016 by The Rosen Publishing Group, Inc.
29 East 21st Street, New York, NY 10010

First Edition

Editor: Caitie McAneney
Book Design: Katelyn Heinle

Photo Credits: Cover, p. 1 BUCHAKA ALEXANDER/Shutterstock.com; cover (series logo coral vector design) Koryaba/Shutterstock.com; back cover mycteria/Shutterstock.com; pp. 3–24 (interior coral vector design) etraveler/Shutterstock.com; pp. 5, 14 © iStockphoto.com/LenaYa; pp. 6, 24 (snout) Jan Zoetekouw/Shutterstock.com; p. 6 (inset) MaxFX/Shutterstock.com; pp. 9, 24 (fin) KAZUHIRO NOGI/AFP/Getty Images; p. 10 Susan E Adams/Flickr.com; pp. 13, 24 (calf) China Photos/Getty Images News/Getty Images; p. 17 Anne Rippy/Photographer's Choice/Getty Images; p. 18 Danita Delimont/Gallo Images/Getty Images; p. 21 Visuals Unlimited, Inc./Solvin Zankl/Visuals Unlimited/Getty Images; p. 22 © iStockphoto.com/Brendan Hunter.

Library of Congress Cataloging-in-Publication Data

Avery, Sebastian, author.
 Porpoises / Sebastian Avery.
     pages cm. — (Ocean friends)
 Includes index.
 ISBN 978-1-5081-4176-1 (pbk.)
 ISBN 978-1-5081-4177-8 (6 pack)
 ISBN 978-1-5081-4178-5 (library binding)
 1. Porpoises—Juvenile literature. I. Title.
 QL737.C434A94 2016
 599.53'9—dc23
                                2015023507

Manufactured in the United States of America

CPSIA Compliance Information: Batch #BW16PK: For Further Information contact Rosen Publishing, New York, New York at 1-800-237-9932

CONTENTS

What's that ocean animal?
It's a porpoise!

dolphin
snout

porpoise snout

Porpoises look a lot like dolphins. However, they don't have long **snouts**.

Porpoises are smaller than most dolphins. They grow about as long as a person is tall.

fin

flipper

10

Porpoises swim with **flippers**. Some have a fin on top of their body.

A mother porpoise has one baby at a time. A baby porpoise is called a **calf**.

Porpoises are smart animals. They use lots of sounds to talk to each other.

Porpoises like to swim together in groups.

There are six different kinds of porpoises. The Dall's porpoise is the fastest.

Harbor porpoises live in the Pacific Ocean. They like to stay close to shore.

This porpoise looks like it's smiling!

WORDS TO KNOW

calf

flipper

snout

INDEX

WEBSITES

Due to the changing nature of Internet links, PowerKids Press has developed an online list of websites related to the subject of this book. This site is updated regularly. Please use this link to access the list: www.powerkidslinks.com/ocea/porp